9/11
101

**101 key points that
everyone should know
and consider that prove
9/11 was an inside job**

Eric D. Williams

First Edition Published January 2006 by

Williamsquire Ltd. Publishing

ISBN 1-4196-2428-8

Cover art designed and created by Eric D. Williams

9/11
101

101 key points that everyone should know and consider that prove 9/11 was an inside job

Eric D. Williams

Dedication

This booklet is dedicated to all those who have lost a member of their family or friend on September 11, 2001 and the pursuing 'war on terrorism.'

May the truth set you free.

Forward

The Puzzle of 9-11 was a great first attempt for me to bring my own questions forward surrounding the events of September 11, 2001.

What has followed was simply unimaginable to me. The dam was broken open and I was connected to many others researching these very same questions. But, my journey was just beginning.

My main problem with my first book was that it was a bit pricy. After continuing my own investigation, I collected the facts about 9/11 and assembled the booklet now before you; 101 facts about September 11. Plane (pun intended) and simple. Of course my own priceless commentary is also included. All wrapped up in an affordable booklet.

The purpose of this booklet is to get it out massively to the general population, and get it out at an affordable price.

It is amazing how so much has happened in the last few years. The more people I meet, the more people are accepting the evidence. When I began my first website questioning the events of 9/11 in November 2001, I was called a lunatic and even unpatriotic. So? Decent is patriotic as is standing up for what you believe! I am glad I am not alone here. But there are still many people who have not seen all the information that blows the 'official story' out of the water. This is the purpose of this booklet!

Enjoy. May the truth start with you!

Eric D. Williams
November 2005
Slovakia

"Today, America would be outraged if U.N. troops entered Los Angeles to restore order. Tomorrow they will be grateful! This is especially true if they were told that there were an outside threat from beyond, whether real or promulgated, that threatened our very existence. It is then that all peoples of the world will plead to deliver them from this evil. The one thing every man fears is the unknown. When presented with this scenario, individual rights will be willingly relinquished for the guarantee of their well-being granted to them by the World Government."
  - Dr. Henry Kissinger, 1991

"We are on the verge of a global transformation. All we need is the right major crisis and the nations will accept the New World Order."
  - David Rockefeller

Class Begins

1) The hijackers' names do not appear on any passenger
list, yet *USA Today*, *NBC*, *BBC* and just about every
other major media source reported which seats the
hijackers had been sitting in. How?

Any crime of such magnitude is subject to extremely
thorough examination by investigative and law
enforcement authorities. In any crime involving the
use of a plane, the obvious first investigative step
taken by the authorities should also then be to find out
who was on the plane.

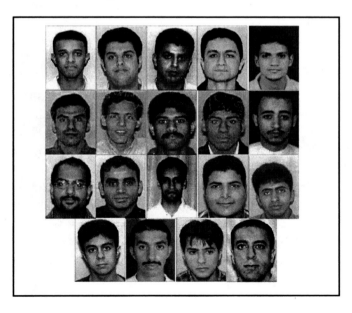

2) The hijackers used false ID's

FBI Director Robert Mueller has acknowledged that some of those behind the 9/11 terror attacks may have stolen the identification of other people, and, according to at least one security expert, it may have been, "Relatively easy" based on their level of sophistication.

Ok, so that explains how they did not appear on any passenger list, but . . .

Airlines keep meticulous records of everyone scheduled to board upon any particular flight. The ID and the type of ID used by anyone on that flight, regardless of whether they used a genuine or fake ID, would therefore be immediately available to the authorities.

3) Discrepancies between the passenger lists

Shortly after the attacks, *CNN* released a partial passenger list from the, "Authorities from American Airlines, United Airlines, the Department of Defense, the New York City Medical Examiners Office and the New York City Fire Department."[1]

In a report for American Airlines Flight 11, this *CNN* report claims that the list states that there were 92 people aboard, yet if you count the names listed there are only 87. Careful reading of the listed passengers reveals no Arabic names.

If you deducted the name of the five suspected hijackers from this list (92 - 87 = 5) this appears to be a reasonable and logical conclusion as the names of the hijackers could have been deleted for security and sensitivity reasons.

Case Closed. Right?

I then checked the passenger list provided by *USA Today*.[2]

Again, another 'partial list.' And this list only contains 86 names and three names that appear on the *CNN* list are missing from the *USA Today* list: Robin Caplin, Jude Larson and Natalie Larson. Yet, the *USA Today* list contains two names that are not on *CNN*'s list: Kelly Booms and Pendyala Vamsikrishna.

So, let's think through the possibility, after all these are 'partial lists' and neither one is complete, that we can add the two names from *USA Today*'s list to *CNN*'s list. This would bring the 'partial list' count to 89. If this is the case, there can't be five hijackers then can there? Yet after almost five years, nobody in the main stream media seems to dispute these discrepancies.

And this is just with Fligh 11. As I pointed out in my first published book *The Puzzle of 9-11*:

"American Airlines Flight 11 has variations of missing between five and eight passengers from the list.

American Airlines Flight 77 has between eight and ten missing names.
United Airlines Flight 175 also had between eight and ten names missing from their list.
United Airlines Flight 93 however, no matter which news website you looked at came up with twelve missing passenger names.

"Going with the lowest number of missing names on the list, the five unaccounted names on Flight 11 confirm that there might have been five hijackers, but the names of the people mentioned in the introduction to this chapter are not named. Flight 77 with a minimum of eight names, gives at least three more helpers on board. And Flight 175 respectfully.
Even Flight 93 had either eight more heroes, or eight more terrorists."[3]

4)   Flight 11, a Boeing 767, could hold 255 yet was only 36% full holding only 92 persons.

5)   Flight 175, a Boeing 767, could also hold 255, yet its capacity was at only 25% with only 65 people on board.

6)   Flight 77, Boeing 757, held only 64 people, 27% of its seating capacity of 239.

7)   Flight 93, another Boeing 757, held the lowest percentage of passengers with only 19% as only 45 persons were on board the plane which cold hold 239.

The number of passengers on these flights compared to other flights during busy weekday flights are incredibly low.

8) If this isn't odd enough, eight of the named hijackers are still alive:

BBC NEWS

You are in: World: Middle East

News Front Page
World

Sunday, 23 September, 2001, 12:30 GMT 13:30 UK

Hijack 'suspects' alive and well

Africa
Americas
Asia-Pacific
Europe
Middle East
South Asia

From Our Own
Correspondent

Letter From
America
UK
England
N Ireland
Scotland

Waleed Al Shehri left the US a year ago, he says

Another of the men named by the FBI as a hijacker in the suicide attacks on Washington and New York has turned up alive and well.

"Saudi Arabian pilot Waleed Al Shehri was one of five men that the FBI said had deliberately crashed American Airlines Flight 11 into the World Trade Centre on 11 September. His photograph was released, and has since appeared in newspapers and on television around the world."[1]

"Some of the men the FBI claims hijacked planes on Sept. 11 and crashed them into the World Trade Center in New York, the Pentagon, and Stony Creek Township, Pennsylvania are still alive. No, they weren't pulled from the rubble - they were never on the planes. The FBI press release of September 27th, 2001 containing names, photographs, aliases and other information is seriously flawed. They have used these peoples names and made claims based on the fact they were pilots ... and other supposedly incriminating evidence ... and yet these men were not involved. Places of birth, birthdays and other personal details were displayed on news throughout the world."[2]

So, again, this raises the false ID questions; "Who's false ID did they use?" And; "Are these false names on the passenger lists or not?"

9) Video surveillance showing Mohammed Atta and Abdulaziz Alomari at the screening station in Portland Airport shows two times: 5:45 and 5:53 (Below).

So what time did they really check in?[1]

In an American Free Press article, U.S. Airways check in agent for more than 37 years, Michael Tuohey, spoke about his brief encounter with Atta and Alomari. He remembered, "Two clean-shaven Arab-looking businessmen with tickets in hand," who approached his workstation, "Both looking elegant and wearing suits and ties." [2]

Did they change clothes between the check in and the screening department? Do you see Arab-looking men, 'Wearing suits and ties,' in the last photograph?

10) US Airways Flight 5930 from Portland to Boston left a window of 15 minutes to board the doomed aircraft. Why would you board a connecting flight with such a little time window?

11) Mohammed Atta's rental car with the incriminating evidence (Arabic language flight materials) was found at Boston Logan Airport.[1] How did he get to Portland to board the plane?

According to the FBI Atta rented another car, a silver-blue Nissan Altima, from an Alamo car rental at Boston's Logan Airport.[2]

Why would Atta leave a rental car containing this incriminating evidence at Logan, rent another car in Boston to drive to Maine, then fly back to Boston again?

12) Atta's luggage, including underwear and a Koran, mysteriously did not make it onto the doomed flight that morning. Why would you pack clothes if you are not planning to be alive later that day? And would not a fundamental Muslim carry his Koran onto the flight he was about to hijack?

FBI seizes records of students at flight schools

"Atta got on the jet off a connecting flight from Portland, Maine. Two bags with Atta's name tags were on the Portland flight, but did not get transferred in time to be loaded on the Los Angeles-bound flight that left Logan Airport at 7:59 a.m., about 45 minutes before it smashed into the World Trade Center tower in New York." - *St. Petersburg Times*

13) NORAD (The North American Aerospace Defense Command) tracks every sky bound object in the skies over North America, even Santa's Christmas Eve delivery route.[1]

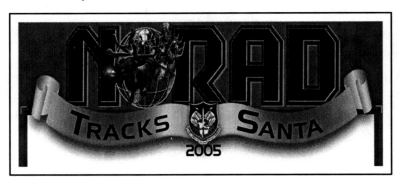

"Deter, Detect, Defend." That is the motto of the men

and women who serve in the North American Aerospace Defense Command. Since 1958, Canadians and Americans have been partners in protecting the airspace of Alaska, Canada and the contiguous 48 United States.[2]

14) When Flight 11 deviated its course, NORAD did not respond.

NORAD spokesman, Maj. Mike Snyder, said they were notified about 10 minutes before Flight 11 hit the World Trade Center.

15) When Flight 175 deviated its course, NORAD again, did not respond.

Richard Meyers, then Acting Chairman of the Joint Chiefs of Staff, in testimony to the Senate Armed Services Committee on September 13, he stated:

"After the second tower was hit, I spoke to the commander of NORAD, General Eberart. And at that point, I think the decision was at that point to start launching aircraft."

16) The beacon of both Flight 11 and 175 were turned off and pilot communication was lost, and NORAD still did not respond.

17) In 1998 Payne Stewart's plane flew off corse and NORAD responded in 20 minutes. Why did NORAD not respond on September 11?

18) When Flight 11 deviated corse, NORAD had 30 minutes to react before it slammed into the WTC.

According to the US Air Force's own website an F-15 routinely, "Goes from scramble order to 29,000 feet in only 2.5 minutes and then can fly at 1,850 nmph (nautical miles per hour)."

19) Knowing that Flight 175 was off corse and something had struck the WTC, NORAD had at least 17 minutes to respond before Flight 175 crashed into the North Tower.

Why did NORAD not respond?

NORAD's, "Fighters routinely intercept aircraft."
- Marine Corps Major Mike Snyder

20) Flight 175 had a tail number of N612UA.

This number is still in use today. This suggests that the plane which struck the WTC North Tower was not Flight 175.

21) What's interesting to note is that the U.S. Government's Bureau of Transportation Statistics (BTS) did not have statistics on their website for the doomed flights of Flight 11 (N334AA), Flight 175

(N612UA), Flight 93 (N591UA), or Flight 77 (N644AA).

So according to the BTS, none of the doomed flights departed on 9/11.

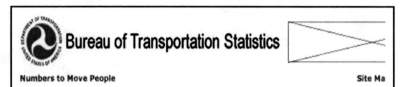

Bureau of Transportation Statistics

Numbers to Move People   Site Ma

Airline On-Time Statistics
Summary Statistics Detailed Statistics Special Reports

Summary Statistics

Airline: American Airlines (AA)
Flight Number: 0011
Time period: September 11, 2001 to September 11, 2001

No data found for the above selection. Please click your browser's Back button or ALT+Left Arrow to return to the previous page and try again.

21) The theories that the planes used were not commercial airliners is also supported due to the bulge or 'pod' attached to the bottom of Flight 175.

In the photo on the following page, notice there is a bulge that is only on the right side of the plane.

This is not a commercial 767 airplane.

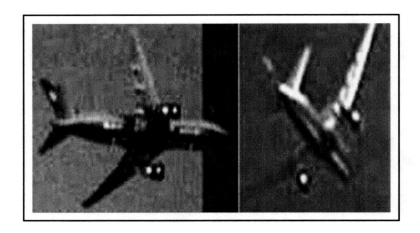

22) From this plane before impact with the tower, a bright flash of light can be seen.

This flash was captured by at least three different angles:

23) Mark Burnback, a Fox News employee, reported: "It definitely didn't look like a commercial plane. I didn't see any windows on the side. Again, it was not a normal flight that I've ever seen at an airport."

24) Wreckage found on the streets of NYC show airplane parts, but not parts belonging to a 757, but a 737.

25) Eye witnesses and early news reports claimed a smaller plane, possibly a commuter plane, had crashed into the North Tower, not a 757 as the official story claims (Flight 11).

26) The only known footage of Flight 11 was captured by the Naudet brothers Gedeon and Jules. The flash (#22) can also be seen as this small plane enters the North Tower.

27) President Bush claimed on *CNN* that he saw the first plane hit the tower.

"QUESTION: How did you feel when you heard about the terrorist attack?"

"BUSH: Well... Well, Jordan (ph), you're not going to believe what state I was in when I heard about the terrorist attack. I was in Florida. And my chief of staff, Andy Card -- actually I was in a classroom talking about a reading program that works. And I was sitting outside the classroom waiting to go in, and I saw an airplane hit the tower -- the TV was obviously on, and I use to fly myself, and I said, "There's one terrible pilot." And I said, "It must have been a horrible accident."

"But I was whisked off there -- I didn't have much time to think about it, and I was sitting in the classroom, and Andy Card, my chief who was sitting over here

14

walked in and said, "A second plane has hit the tower. America's under attack."

This is impossible because no news cameras were at the scene at this time, and no live feeds were running to the news channels before the crash of the first plane, after all, it was a surprise attack. How could he have seen this plane hit the towers?

Also, to assume that an aircraft slamming into the WTC in postcard perfect weather was pilot error is absolutely absurd. The only other known impact involving a New York City skyscraper was on July 28, 1945, when a ten-ton, B-25 bomber smashed into the north side of the Empire State Building due to heavy fog. The plane hit the 79th floor, creating a hole in the building eighteen feet wide and twenty feet high.

Impact on the Empire State Building in 1945

It must be remembered that even after Andrew Card whispered into Bush's ear of the second plane's impact, and according to his own admission Bush was told America was, "Under attack," he continued to stay in the classroom full of children for 20 minutes.

29) President Bush was in his limo when told about the first plane crashing.

"The President was on Highway 301, just north of Main Street ... [when] he received the news that a plane had crashed in New York City."[1]

"Bush was driving to the school in a motorcade when the phone rang. An airline accident appeared to have happened. He pressed on with his visit."[2]

30) Radio-controlled aircraft have been used by NASA at least since 1984. In an online article about their tests they report:

"Before the final flight on December 1, 1984, more than four years of effort passed trying to set-up final impact conditions.

"NASA Dryden developed the remote piloting techniques necessary for the B-720 to fly as a drone aircraft.

"The 15 flights had 15 takeoffs, 14 landings and a larger number of approaches to about 150 feet above the prepared crash site under remote control.

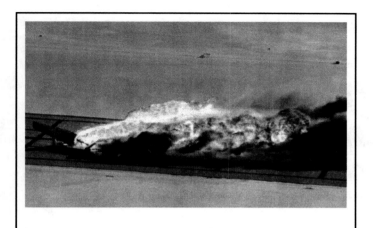

Dryden Flight Research Center EC84-31809 Photographed 1984
Remotely piloted Boeing 720 Controlled Impact Demonstration
aircraft following impact with iron cutter posts. NASA photo

"On the final flight (No. 15) with no crew, all fuel tanks were filled with a total of 76,000 pounds of AMK and the remotely-piloted aircraft landed on Rogers Dry Lakebed in an area prepared with posts to test the effectiveness of the AMK in a controlled impact.

"The CID, which some wags called the Crash in the Desert, was spectacular with a large fireball enveloping and burning the B-720 aircraft."

31) 'Planes Don't Blow Up' Aviation Experts Assert'

"BOSTON--Airplane design is a craft of precision, computer projections and reassuring statistics. Blowing a plane from the sky is a chaotic act of evil intent, slim opportunity and hellish luck.

'Planes Don't Blow Up,' Aviation Experts Assert

Only a Very Well Placed Bomb Could Do It

By Fred Bayles
The Associated Press

BOSTON — Airplane design is a craft of precision, computer projections and reassuring statistics. Blowing a plane from the sky is a chaotic act of evil intent, slim opportunity and hellish luck.

This is why, beyond the awful loss of 230 lives, aeronautics and terrorism experts are so disturbed by the explosion of TWA 800.

For them, the mystery of what happened at 13,700 feet stirs special dread: They see either a mechanical failure unlike anything experienced or a terrorist act of accuracy and precision rarely seen.

in 1991 when a computer error caused one engine to deploy its reverse thruster, sending the plane into a vicious spin.

But in neither case was there a cataclysmic explosion.

Before TWA 800 went down last week, there had never been an explosion of such ferocity aboard a 747-100, a "wet-wing," or plane that carries all its fuel in wing tanks.

"You have to have instant ignition into a large fuel source," said Mr. Barr, who trains accident investigators. "The way those fuel tanks are sealed, it just doesn't happen."

Few bombings of commercial aircraft have ended in such a fiery conclusion. In many cases, jetliners have survived even severe

---

"This is why, beyond the awful loss of 230 lives, aeronautics and terrorism experts are so disturbed by the explosion of TWA 800.

"For them, the mystery of what happened at 13,700 feet stirs special dread: They see either a mechanical failure unlike anything experienced or a terrorist act of accuracy and precision rarely seen.

"If it was an accident, it would scare the hell out of us," said Michael Barr, director of aviation safety programs at the University of Southern California. "These planes just don't blow up. There's too many fire walls, too

18

many checks and balances.'

"Christopher Ronay is equally troubled. As head of the FBI bomb unit for seven years, he investigated 30aircraft bombings before retiring in 1994. "I can't recall anything that has had a catastrophic effect like this case," he said. "You could blow the hell out of a cargo compartment with a luggage bomb, but you have to blow up a fuel cell or an engine to get an explosion like that."

"Their perplexed fears are based on witness accounts of a huge orange fireball, a possible marker of exploding jet fuel. The Boeing 747 had taken off just 12 minutes before, its tanks loaded with 48,445 gallons of fuel for the long flight to France.

"The specific fuel involved is called Jet A, a derivative of kerosene and a sluggish explosive. To explode, it must mix with air, an indication that one or more of the eight fuel cells in the jumbo jet's wings were breached--either by violent engine or mechanical failure, by a well- bomb or possibly by a missile.

"Before TWA 800 went down last week, there had never been an explosion of such ferocity aboard a 747-100, a 'wet-wing,' or plane that carries all its fuel in wing tanks.

"You have to have instant ignition into a large fuel source," said Mr. Barr, who trains accident investigators. "The way those fuel tanks are sealed, it just doesn't happen."

"Few bombings of commercial aircraft have ended in such a fiery conclusion. In many cases, jetliners have survived even severe damage from explosions and landed safely.

"In 1986, terrorists planted a sheet of plastic explosive the size of a business letter under one seat on a TWA flight from Rome to Athens. The explosion killed one man, blowing his seat out of the plane. A grandmother, daughter and grandchild were sucked out of the resulting hole. But the plane survived."

32) The WTC North Tower, which was struck at 8:45 a.m. around the 93rd floor, burned for 1 hour 44 minutes before it collapsed at about 10:29 a.m.

33) The WTC South Tower which was struck at 9:03 a.m. at about the 80th floor, collapsed about 9:50 a.m. after only 47 minutes ablaze.

34) No steel building in history has ever collapsed due to fire before or after 9/11.

Los Angeles 1988

"During the late evening of May 4, 1988, and the early morning of May 5, 1988, members of the Los Angeles City Fire Department successfully battled what has proven to be the worst, most devastating high-rise fire in the history of Los Angeles.

"Extinguishing this blaze at the 62-story First Interstate Bank Building, 707 West Wilshire Boulevard, required the combined efforts of 64 fire companies, 10 City rescue ambulances, 17 private ambulances, 4 helicopters, 53 Command Officers and support personnel, a complement of 383 Firefighters and Paramedics, and considerable assistance from other City departments."

Philadelphia 1991
On February 23, 1991 at approximately 8:40pm, the Meridian Bank Building, also known as One Meridian Plaza in Philadelphia, a 38-story office building, caught fire.

The fire, which blazed on eight floors for more than nineteen hours, caused three firefighter fatalities and injuries to 24 firefighters. 51 engine companies, 15 ladder companies, 11 specialized units responded, and more than 300 firefighters arrived on the scene.

It was the largest high-rise office building fire in modern American history, until 9/11, completely consuming eight floors of the building.

The blaze was eventually contained and extinguished,

yet it did not bring down the building.

Madrid 2005

"On the evening of Saturday February 12, 2005 a fire broke out in the Windsor tower in Madrid, Spain. The building is located in the heart of Madrid's commercial and banking centre and is one of the tallest in the capital.

"The control room in the basement of the building registered a fire signal from the 21st Floor at 23:05 on the night of Saturday 12 February 2005.

"A time of 16 minutes elapsed between this signal and the call being made to the Fire Brigade - who arrived on site at 23:25. Security personnel claim that a time of 10 – 15 minutes elapsed from Fire Brigade arrival to first fire attack i.e. 30 – 35 minutes after the initial alarm was registered in the control room.

"By about 01:15 the fire had spread to most of the floors above the 21st Floor, resulting in a 10-storey blaze. Soon afterwards the first chunks of facade started falling off, taking the perimeter bay of the RC slab with it in places. The spread of fire downwards was gradual at first, probably due to burning embers dropping through services penetrations, through slab edge openings and through other openings in the concrete slabs caused by core wall expansion.

"A thermo-mechanical assessment of this structural design, an understanding of why the structure performed as it did and why total collapse did not occur would provide valuable information for future structural fire analysis in design."

35) At 5:25 p.m. on September 11, 2001, WTC 7, a 47-story office building, collapsed symmetrically. This building was built on top of an electrical substation which housed ten large electrical transformers. Fuel tanks with the capacity of 42,000 gallons were also installed to supply emergency power to the building.

Why were so many emergency power applications placed into this building?

Mayor Giuliani had created a $13 million emergency control bunker to carry out executive orders during an emergency in New York City.

Oddly enough, according to NYFD transcripts, WTC 7

was not reported to be on fire until 3 p.m., five hours after the Twin Towers had collapsed.

36) Larry Silverstein, owner of the WTC Complex stated in the PBS documentary, *America Rebuilds*:

"And I remember getting a call from the, uh, fire department commander, telling me that they were not sure they were gonna be able to contain the fire,

and I said, 'well, you know, we've had such terrible loss of life, maybe the smartest thing to do is, is PULL it.'"

And he continued:

"And they made that decision to pull and then we watched the building collapse."

Later in the same documentary, a construction worker refers to the demolition of WTC 6:

"We're getting ready to pull the building six."

There can be little doubt as to how the word "pull" is being used in this context.

37) Silverstein bought the complex for $200 million in

May 2001. He then purchased huge amounts of insurance on the property and after the attacks collected $3.5 billion, but wanted $7 billion stating it was two separate attacks. Usually, when someone purchases property, then purchases mass amounts of insurance before its destruction and then later collects more that the property's value, is a criminal suspect.

Why not this time?

38) **Law of Falling bodies**

Distance (d) = (32.16/2) x Time in Seconds Squared. WTC is 1353 feet tall.

1353 = (32.16/2) x Time in Seconds Squared. This works out to 9.1627 seconds as the fastest time these buildings could come down without resistance, i.e. the tower below.

39) The WTC South Tower fell in 10.4 seconds.

40) The WTC North Tower fell in 8.1 seconds.

Both towers had plenty of resistance. The resistance was the enormous lower sections of the building that were not effected by the airplanes.

If a pancake collapse had truly occurred, the resistance below would have actually slowed the fall of the building down, not speed it up.

The times in which both towers fell defies the laws of gravity!

41) WTC 7 collapsed in 6.5 seconds. 0.5 seconds faster than free-fall. And remember nothing impacted this building.

42) Jet fuel, which is only refined kerosene, when mixed properly, burns briefly at 1800 degrees F. The color of the burning jet fuel is amber, not bright red as was the color at the WTC.

43) Steel, which is about 99% iron, melts at 2800 °F or 1538 °C.

44) When the World Trade Towers were built in the 1970s, at 110 storeys and 1350 feet it was the tallest building that had ever been built. Please consider that the architectural engineers, suppliers, builders, and city inspectors were very careful to overbuild every aspect.

The WTC was built using 47 interior core columns (No 17, image next page) and not to mention 236 large exterior fire coated steel columns (No 13).

The interior columns and the exterior columns were welded and bolted together with steel plates. Steel trusses were crisscrossed between the columns creating a mesh network that bound the WTC together. Corrugated pans (No 20) were also assembled in which concrete was poured into them on every floor to create a deep and solid foundation.

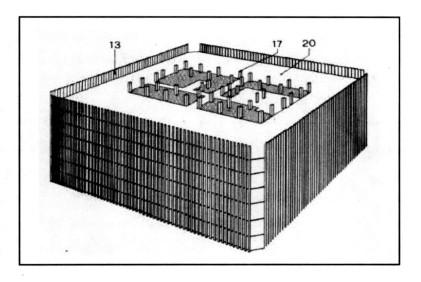

This design also incorporated the ability to absorb energy and to sway in storms.

One of the lead engineers who designed the World Trade Center Towers, Lee Robertson, expressed shock that the towers collapsed after being hit by the passenger jets:

"I designed it for a 707 to hit it."[1]

The Boeing 707 has a fuel capacity of more than 23,000 gallons,[2] comparable to the 767's 23,980-gallon fuel capacity.[3]

45) We were told that the WTC collapsed because of the intense heat created by the jet fuel. How does the jet stay in flight for up to 10 hours with their engines burning at 1800 D F, yet the WTC burned at 1200 for less than 2 hours?

46) *People Weekly Magazine* on September 24, 2001 reported that one of the first firefighters in the second tower, Louie Cacchioli, 51:

> jumped from the building. ... the floating bodies. It was like they were in slow motion, sort of turning around. You had to think there must have been such total desperation.
>
> **Louie Cacchioli, 51, is a firefighter assigned to Engine 47 in Harlem.**
>
> We were the first ones in the second tower after the plane struck. I was taking firefighters up in the elevator to the 24th floor to get in position to evacuate workers. On the last trip up a bomb went off. We think there was bombs set in the building. I had just asked another firefighter to stay with me, which was a good thing because we were trapped inside the elevator and he had the tools to get out.
>
> There were probably 500 people trapped in the stairwell. It was mass chaos. The power went out. It was dark. Everybody was screaming. We had oxygen masks and we were giving people

"I was taking firefighters up in the elevator to the 24th floor to get in position to evacuate workers. On the last trip up a bomb went off. We think there were bombs set in the building."

47) Kim White, 32, an employee on the 80th floor, also reported hearing an explosion. "All of a sudden the building shook, then it started to sway. We didn't know what was going on," she told *People*. "We got all our people on the floor into the stairwell . . . at that time we all thought it was a fire . . .We got down as far as the 74th floor . . . then there was another explosion."

48) In the Naudet Brothers' documentary film *9/11*, two firefighters stated:

Fireman2: We made it outside, we made it about a block.

Fireman1: We made it at least 2 blocks.

Fireman2: 2 blocks.

Fireman1: and we started runnin'

Fireman2: poch-poch-poch-poch-poch-poch-poch

Fireman1: Floor by floor it started poppin' out ..

Fireman2: It was as if as if they had detonated, det..

Fireman1: yea detonated yea

Fireman2: as if they had planned to take down a building, boom boom boom boom boom boom boom boom ...

Fireman1: All the way down, I was watchin it, and runnin'.

49) "It actually gave at a lower floor, not the floor where the plane hit, because we originally had thought there was like an internal detonation explosives because it went in succession, boom, boom, boom, boom, and then the tower came down."

50) **Basement janitor hero on 9/11**

"WTC janitor pulls burn victim to safety after basement explosion rocks North Tower seconds before jetliner hit top floors. Also, two other men trapped and drowning in a basement elevator shaft, were also pulled to safety from underground explosion..

"Declared a hero for saving numerous lives at Ground Zero, he was the janitor on duty the morning of 9/11 who heard and felt explosions rock the basement sub-levels of the north tower just seconds before the jetliner struck the top floors.

He not only claims he felt explosions coming from below the first sub-level while working in the basement, he says the walls were cracking around him and he pulled a man to safety by the name of Felipe David, who was severely burned from the basement explosions."

All these events occurred only seconds *before* and during Flight 11's strike from above. And through it all, he now asks a very simple question everybody should be asking? How could a jetliner hit 90 floors above and burn a man's arms and face to a crisp in the basement below seconds before and after the impact?

51) There can be seen plumes of smoke, similar to demolition charges being set off, coming from below the collapsing tower.

52) A reporter for *USA Today* stated that the FBI believed that bombs in the buildings brought the buildings down;

"The NY Fire Department Chief of Safety stated there were "bombs" and "secondary devices," which caused the explosions in the buildings;

"A NYC firefighters who witnessed attacks stated that it looked like there were bombs in the buildings;

"An MSNBC reporter stated that police had found a suspicious device "and they fear it could be something that might lead to another explosion" and the police officials believe "that one of the explosions at the world trade center . . . may have been caused by a van that was parked in the building that may have had some kind of explosive device in it, so their fear is that there may have been explosive devices planted either in the building or in the adjacent area";

"A NYC firefighter stated "the south tower . . . exploded . . . At that point a debate began to rag e because the perception was that the building looked like it had been taken out with charges . . . many people had felt that possibly explosives had taken out 2 World Trade";

"Assistant Fire Commissioner stated "I thought . . . before . . . No. 2 came down, that I saw low-level flashes. . . . I . . . saw a flash flash flash . . . [at] the lower level of the building [not up where the fire was]. You know like when they . . . blow up a building ... ?" -- and a lieutenant firefighter the Commissioner spoke with independently verified the flashes;

"A firefighter said "[T]here was just an explosion. It seemed like on television [when] they blow up these buildings. It seemed like it was going all the way around like a belt, all these explosions"; Another firefigther stated "it almost sounded like bombs going off, like boom, boom, boom, like seven or eight";

"A paramedic said "at first I thought it was -- do you ever see professional demolition where they set the charges on certain floors and then you hear pop pop pop pop pop -- thats exactly what because thought it was";

"A police officer noted "People were saying, 'There's another one and another one.' I heard reports of secondary bomb explosions ...";

"A firefighter stated "there was an explosion in the south tower, which . . . just blew out in flames . . . One floor under another after another and when it hit about the fifth floor, I figured it was a bomb, because it looked like a synchronized deliberate kind of thing. I was there in '93" (referring to 1993 bombing of world trade center);

"A firefighter stated "it looked like sparkling around one specific layer of the building . . . Then the building started to come down. My initial reaction was that this was exactly the way it looks when they show you those implosions on TV";

"Dan Rather said that collapse was "reminiscent of those pictures we've all seen [when] a building was deliberately destroyed by well-placed dynamite to knock it down."

53) Marvin Bush, President Bush's brother, is co-owner of the company that provided security for the WTC Complex.

54) During controlled Demolition, charges are placed so that the steel beams

can be easily loaded onto trailers to be carried away.

This was exactly the case at the WTC. Many beams were found measuring 30 feet in length.

55) Without an investigation underway, the steel at the WTC was shipped of to China and India to be melted and recycled.[1]

When the Federal Emergency Management Agency (FEMA) was then given the job of investigating the collapse of the WTC, issued in its report in May of 2002, it declares that "the sequence of events leading to the collapse of each tower could not be definitely determined."[2]

Plumes of smoke point to demolition charges.

56) The concrete was not in chunks, but pulverized into very small particles. The massive energy required to pulverize concrete suggests the use of explosives throughout the building.

57) When comparing the damage with what one plane was reported to have done at the WTC with what happened at the Pentagon, which 'coincidentally' broke

ground on September 11, 1941, the damage is not
even comparable.

58) Smoke damage was minimal at the Pentagon. Even windows were unbroken near the impact area.

Notice how white the walls

59) No 757 aircraft parts were found at the Pentagon. No wings, no tail, no seats, no luggage, no plane.

60) Blueprints of the Pentagon show the windows were 5 feet across. So based on this knowledge, the initial hole at the Pentagon was between 14 - 16 feet.

61) A 757 has a wingspan measuring 124' 10", a length of 155' 3", and a tail height, with landing gear extended, 44' 6". The 757's fuselage's width measures 12' 4".

How does an airplane with these measurements fit into a hole measuring 14 - 16 feet and not leave any wreckage?

Please look carefully at the following photo. Where is the plane's wreckage?

62) The moves reported are impossible for an airplane of this size at the reported speeds.

One witness described a plane at several thousand feet making a combined dive and a 270° turn bringing the plane to street level.

CBS News reported:

"At 9:33 the plane crossed the Capitol Beltway and took aim on its military target. But the jet, flying at more than 400 mph, was too fast and too high when it neared the Pentagon at 9:35. The hijacker-pilots were then forced to execute a difficult high-speed descending turn.

"Radar shows Flight 77 did a downward spiral, turning almost a complete circle and dropping the last 7,000 feet in two-and-a-half minutes.

"The steep turn was so smooth, the sources say, it's clear there was no fight for control going on. And the complex maneuver suggests the hijackers had better flying skills than many investigators first believed."

This photo compares the path of 'Flight 77' yet no wing damage is visible where the plane supposedly hit.

63) Renovation of the Pentagon had begun earlier in 2001. The side renovated first was the side impacted on 9/11. Therefore, under renovation, most of the offices were absent of people and this reduced the number of casualties.

Would hijackers not want to aim for the area of the building which was weaker and contained the most amounts of people, including important persons like Donald Rumsfeld, or others?

Please remember that more than 25,000 civilians and military personnel work at the Pentagon.

64) As with Flight 175, Flight 77 tail number, N644AA is still in use.

65) An eye witness at the Pentagon Mike Walter told CNN that what he saw:

"Was like a cruise missile with wings, went right there and slammed into the Pentagon. Huge explosion, great ball of fire, smoke started billowing out, and then it was just chaos on the highway."

This is what a small commuter plane looks like when it slams into a brick building. Why is there not similar damage or wreckage in photos of the Pentagon?

66) *The Washington Post* spoke to Steve Patterson, who said that he saw the plane from about 150 yards away, "Approaching from the west about 20 feet off the ground." He then described the plane as having, "The high-pitched squeal of a fighter jet," and said that it, "Flew over Arlington cemetery so low that he thought it was going to land on I-385. He said it was flying so fast that he couldn't read any writing on the side." Patterson also stated the aircraft that he saw, "Appeared to hold about eight to 12 people."

There is a sufficient size difference between a plane which holds eight to twelve people and a 757.

67) CNN correspondent Jamie McIntyre reporting live from the Pentagon stating that there was no evidence of a plane having crashed anywhere near the building.

JAMIE MCINTYRE:

"From my close-up inspection there's no evidence of a plane having crashed anywhere near the Pentagon.

"The only site, is the actual side of the building that's crashed in.

And as I said, the only pieces left that you can see are small enough that you pick up in your hand.

"There are no large tail sections, wing sections, fuselage, nothing like that anywhere around which would indicate that the entire plane crashed into the side of the Pentagon and then caused the side to collapse.

"Even though if you look at the pictures of the Pentagon you see that the floors have all collapsed, that didn't happen immediately. It wasn't until almost about 45 minutes later that the structure was weakened enough that all of the floors collapsed."

68) Video surveillance tapes from local businesses were confiscated on 9/11. If these videos had shown Flight

77 impacting the Pentagon, we would have seen them numerous times. So, what do these video show?

Also remember that Washington D.C. has more camera and surveillance equipment around the area than any other place in America. So when the military only releases only five photos of the impact, is it not a wise question to ask where are the other images of the 757 attacking the Pentagon?

Sep. 12, 2001, 17:37:19   impact Sep. 12, 2001, 17:37:23   #4 impact

69) In a slip of the tongue, Donald Rumsfeld claimed a missile had hit the Pentagon.

"It is a truth that a terrorist can attack any time, any place, using any technique and it's physically impossible to defend at every time and every place against every conceivable technique. Here we're talking about plastic knives and using an American Airlines flight filled with our citizens, and the missile to damage this building and similar (inaudible) that damaged the World Trade Center. The only way to deal with this problem is by taking the battle to the terrorists, wherever they are, and dealing with them."

70) Very much resembling a small passenger plane or military jet, The Global Hawk Unmanned Aerial Vehicle is literally as Mike Walter said "a cruise missile with wings."

How it operates is explained by the Federation of American Scientists:

"After launch, the missile's folded wings, tail surfaces and engine inlet deploy. It is then able to fly complicated routes to a target through the use of an onboard Global Positioning System (GPS) coupled with its Inertial Navigation System (INS). This allows the missile to guide itself to the target with pinpoint accuracy."

71) No Muslim DNA was found at the Pentagon.

72) Flight 93 was reported to have cashed because of the heroic deeds of the passengers.

It was also reported that they decided to do something about their hijacked airplane because of the cell phone calls they placed.

Cell phones do not work on airplanes at that high of altitude.

"K. Dewdney, Professor Emeritus at the University of Western Ontario, has released the results of the third and concluding experiment in the "Project Achilles" series, that concludes that cellphone calls, allegedly made from "hijacked" airplanes on September 11th 2001, was impossible. The physical impossibility of the cellphone calls, widely reported in the American media, calls into question the whole Osama Bin Asset story put forward by the American government and press."

73) As with the Pentagon, no plane wreckage was found at the 'crash site' of Flight 93 in Pennsylvania.

Although: "Eight miles away in New Baltimore, Melanie Hankinson said she found singed papers and other light debris from the crash, including pages from Hemispheres Magazine, United's in-flight magazine."

Could debris from a crash site that contains no plane wreckage have traveled over a mountain ridge more than eight miles?

The following photos compare the photo taken of the
smoke from Flight 93 (1) with the photo taken of a
missile launched and crashed in Iraq(2).

74) Eyewitnesses claimed to have seen a second jet in the
sky:

"In separate interviews Thursday, five residents who
live and work less than four miles from the crash site
said they saw a second plane flying erratically within
minutes of the crash of the Boeing 757 that took off
from Newark two hours earlier Tuesday morning.

"Susan Mcelwain of Stonycreek Township said a small
white jet with rear engines and no discernible
markings swooped low over her minivan near an
intersection and disappeared over a hilltop, nearly
clipping the tops of trees lining the ridge.

"It was less than a minute later, Mcelwain said, that
the ground shook and a white plume of smoke

appeared over the ridge. "It was so close to me I ducked," Mcelwain said. "I heard it hit and saw the smoke. All I could think of was how close I came to dying. " About a mile north on Buckstown Road, Dennis Decker and Rick Chaney were at work making wooden pallets when they heard an explosion and came running outside to watch a large mushroom cloud spreading over the ridge.

"As soon as we looked up, we saw a midsized jet flying low and fast," Decker said. "It appeared to make a loop or part of a circle, and then it turned fast and headed out. " Decker and Chaney described the plane as a Lear-jet type, with engines mounted near the tail and painted white with no identifying markings.

"If you were here to see it, you'd have no doubt," Decker said. "It was a jet plane, and it had to be flying real close when that 757 went down. If I was the FBI, I'd find out who was driving that plane. " Late Thursday afternoon, federal agents who spoke to reporters at the crash site said "there was no evidence as of yet" that a second plane was nearby when Flight 93 plunged into a strip mine.

75) Please notice the picture on the next page: The crash site is a 'crater' approximately 70 feet across. Notice all the unburned grass and the green trees so close to the alleged impact point.

Just as with the Pentagon, there is no evidence what so ever of any aircraft wreckage. No wings. No tail. No engines. No Flight 93.

There also is no evidence of any aircraft tearing down trees in its 'nose-dive.'

76) Residents in the area of the crash reported TV's and other electronic devices flickering before hearing a loud boom.

This is typical of a shoot down as an EMP (Electro Magnetic Pulse) is fired to lock the targeting system onto its target.

Some eyewitnesses also reported that the lights at Indian Lake Marina flickered just before hearing the explosion that preceded the sighting of falling debris.

There are three possible actions in a shoot-down scenario that would be consistent with both the flickering lights and the sequence of events. The first is that stray rounds from the aircraft cannon struck an electric line somewhere in the vicinity. The second is that a fighter jet maneuvered so low to the ground that its "wake turbulence" actually shook the power line. The third is that the interceptor used an EMP weapon to momentarily disrupt the airliner's controls, and that weapon disturbed electrical circuits on the ground.

We might never know which of those possibilities is correct, just as we might never get access to all of the government's information about what really happened that day. But, one thing continues to become clearer: the government-sponsored story does not fit the evidence, and it does not make sense in light of national policy on dealing with terrorists.

77) On 9/11, WCPO Channel 9 in Cincinnati ran a story stating that Flight 93 and Flight 175 had landed at Cleveland because of bomb threats.

"On the morning of 9/11 a little known Cincinnati television station ran a story saying Flight 93 landed at Cleveland International Airport instead of crashing into the Pentagon as claimed in the official government story.

"Reporters at WCPO Channel 9 quoted then Cleveland Mayor Michael R. White as saying "a Boeing 767 out of Boston made an emergency landing due to a bomb threat," the airplane landing safely, moved to a secure location and evacuated.

"The early morning report went on to say United Airlines verified the plane as Flight 93, but was also deeply concerned about another jetliner in the vicinity, Flight 175, flying from Boston to Los Angeles.

"Also included in the little known news report was a comment from United CEO, James Goodwin, who said, "The thoughts of everyone at United are with the passengers and crew of these flights. Our prayers are also with everyone on the ground who may have been involved. United Airlines is working with all the relevant authorities, including the FBI, to obtain further information on these flights."

"Former Mayor White, as well as United and WCPO, could not be reached for comment, but the evidence still remains, even though it was suspiciously removed from the television's web site in June 2004 in and around the time of the 9/11 Commission hearings.

"With the evidence trail getting colder and colder, the obvious still must be asked: if Flight 175 was slamming into the South Tower and Flight 93 was downed over Pennsylvania like the government contends, why did Mayor White say that both planes were in or in the vicinity of Cleveland?"

78) Two 911 Planes Were Never De-registered

"Two of the 9/11 airliners were never 'deregistered' and remained on the 'active' flight list until Sept. 28. 2005, the classification officially changing only a month after two inquisitive flight researchers made repeated calls to the Federal Aviation Administration (FAA), inquiring about the strange irregularity.

"The two planes in question were Flight 93 and Flight 175, both owned and operated by United Airlines and, according to the official story, both destroyed on 9/11, one in Shanksville, Penn., and the other crashing into the South Tower of the WTC.

"Usually a normal procedure after an airliner is destroyed, why it took United more than four years to 'deregister' the airplanes and fill out the official FAA paperwork remains a mystery and never has been fully explained by the FAA, United or the government.

"In fact, in stark contrast, a check of FAA records shows the two other American Airline flights, Flight 11 and 77, both were 'deregistered' and classified as 'destroyed' only months after 9/11 on Jan. 14, 2002."

79) While all this was going on, President Bush was patiently reading with school children at Booker Elementary School in Florida. The presidents whereabouts were widely reported days in advance.

Why didn't the FBI nor the Secret Service not think that the President was in any danger and escort him off to safety?

The President was also scheduled to address the media

that morning at precisely 9:30. His message, although altered by the unfolding events, arrived on cue.

80) After the reported panicky fly from here to there adventures of the President and Air Force One,[1] when landing safely on the White House lawn Bush proudly proclaimed "Its over."[2]

How did he know that the terrorists had finished their jobs and that more attacks were not planned?

81) One week before the attacks, stock options were placed on both American Airlines and United Airlines. In fact, there was an increase of 1200% in trading activities for their stocks to go 'short.' An investor places a 'short' on a stock when he expects that stock to go down in value.

"In the days before the terrorist assaults, unusually high numbers of put options were purchased for the stocks of AMR Corp. and UAL Corp., the parents of American and United - each of which had two planes hijacked."[1]

The short selling of American and United Airlines' stocks of on the New York Stock Exchange prior to 9/11 resulted in $2.5 million in profits after United stock dropped 43 percent and American dropped 39 percent the first day the market reopened after the attack.

"Chicago traders on Wednesday cited unusual activity in airline options up to a month before attacks on U.S.

landmarks, and German bankers reported brisk activity in reinsurer Munich Re shares, adding to speculation that those behind the attacks tried to profit from their acts.

"In Frankfurt, bankers also noticed unusual interest in stock-lending in shares of Munich Re, raising the possibility that at least one player may have prepared a short position with advance knowledge of an attack that would send the insurer's shares plummeting."[2]

Many of the profits made by these shares are still unclaimed.[3]

After 9/11, both the SEC and the Secret Service announce investigations into the unusually high volume trade of five-year US Treasury note purchases. These transactions include a single $5 billion trade.

"A broad government inquiry into whether anyone with prior knowledge profited from the Sept. 11 attacks widened to include suspicious trading in the Treasury bond market.

"Investigators from the U.S. Secret Service contacted a number of bond traders regarding large purchases of five-year Treasury notes before the attacks, according to people familiar with the probe. The investigators, acting on a tip from traders, are examining whether terrorists, or people affiliated with terrorist organizations, bought five-year notes, including a single $5 billion trade, the people say.

"Five-year Treasury notes are among the best investments in the event of a world crisis, especially one that hits the U.S. The notes are prized for their safety and their backing by the U.S. government, and usually rally when investors flee riskier investments, such as stocks. Since the attacks, the notes have posted a return of 2.5%. Returns could have been far greater since many big bond investors turn to the futures market, where they use leverage, or borrowed money, to amplify their gains."[4]

82) John Ashcroft; Willie Brown, Mayor of San Francisco; Shalmon Rustie, author, all stopped flying on commercial airliners before the attacks:

Ashcroft stopped flying on July 26, 2001

Fishing rod in hand, Attorney General John Ashcroft left on a weekend trip to Missouri Thursday afternoon aboard a chartered government jet.

"There was a threat assessment and there are guidelines. He is acting under the guidelines," an FBI spokesman said. Neither the FBI nor the Justice Department, however, would identify what the threat was, when it was detected or who made it.[1]

Eight hours prior to the attacks, San Francisco Mayor Willie Brown received a warning from "my security people at the airport," advising him to be cautious in traveling.

"The mayor, who was booked to fly to New York yesterday morning from San Francisco International Airport, said the call "didn't come in any alarming fashion, which is why I'm hesitant to make an alarming statement."[2]

Salman Rushdie, author of *The Satanic Verses* - a satyrical portrayal of Islamic faith, said he believes the authorities knew the attack was coming.

The Times of London reported, "On September 3 (2001) the Federal Aviation Authority made an emergency ruling to prevent Mr Rushdie from flying unless airlines complied with strict and costly security measures. Mr Rushdie told The Times that the airlines would not upgrade their security."[3]

The FAA later confirmed that it had in fact banned Rushdie from flying in the US and Canada but refused to say why.

83) Area NYC Schools and businesses, including the WTC, were half empty on the day of the attacks.

A Pakistani student attending New Utrecht High School, in Brooklyn, New York City, about one week before 9/11, pointed at the WTC and declared, "Look at those two buildings. They won't be here next week."[1]

"Jersey City school administrators confirmed that several days before the attack, a student of Middle Eastern descent issued a vague warning not to travel into lower Manhattan the morning of Sept. 11."[2]

"A Seattle man of Middle Eastern descent who reportedly predicted terrorists would attack the United States has been subpoenaed by a federal grand jury in New York, according to sources familiar with the investigation.

"The man, employed as a security guard, suggested to an East Coast friend in a telephone conversation days before the Sept. 11 passenger-jet hijackings that an attack on U.S. soil was coming, the sources said."[3]

A *Village Voice* reporter is told by a New York taxi driver, "You know, I am leaving the country and going home to Egypt sometime in late August or September. I have gotten e-mails from people I know saying that

Osama bin Laden has planned big terrorist attacks for New York and Washington for that time. It will not be safe here then." He did in fact return to Egypt.[4]

84) FEMA, The Federal Emergency Management Agency, who responds to hurricanes, tornadoes, and other National emergencies, arrived the day before the attacks.

Speaking with Dan Rather on September 12, 2001, FEMA spokesman Tom Kenney states that FEMA was deployed to New York on Monday night, September 10th, to be ready to go into action on Tuesday morning, September 11th.

"We're currently one of the first teams that was deployed to support the city of New York for this disaster. We arrived on late Monday night, and went into action on Tuesday morning. And not until today did we get a full opportunity to work the entire site."

Again I thought this was a surprise attack?

85) In July 2001, Bush singed W1-99i which told FBI investigators to back off the Bin Laden investigation.

"Newsnight has obtained evidence that the FBI was on the trail of other members of the] Bin Laden family for links to terrorist organization before and after September 11th.

This document is marked "Secret". Case ID - 199-Eye W.F. 213 589. 199 is FBI code for case type. 9 would be murder. 65 would be espionage. 199 means national security. W.F. indicates Washington field office special agents were investigating ABC - because of it's relationship with the World Assembly of Muslim Youth, AMY - a suspected terrorist organization. ABL is Abdullah Bin Laden, president and treasurer of WAMY."

86) FBI Agent John O'Neil, who resigned from the FBI because of this order from Bush, received a new job as head of security at the World Trade Center Complex making $350,000 a year job. His first day on the job was September 10.

His body was found on top of the smoldering rubble at Ground Zero.

87) Terror Drills for the exact same scenarios had been taking place years before and 'coincidentally' on the same day.

1999 - NORAD starts conducting exercises in which airplanes are hijacked and crashed into targets which include the World Trade Center and the Pentagon.

"In the two years before the Sept. 11 attacks, the North American Aerospace Defense Command conducted exercises simulating what the White House says was unimaginable at the time: hijacked airliners used as weapons to crash into targets and cause mass casualties.

"One of the imagined targets was the World Trade

Center. In another exercise, jets performed a mock shoot-down over the Atlantic Ocean of a jet supposedly laden with chemical poisons headed toward a target in the United States. In a third scenario, the target was the Pentagon — but that drill was not run after Defense officials said it was unrealistic, NORAD and Defense officials say.

"NORAD, in a written statement, confirmed that such hijacking exercises occurred. It said the scenarios outlined were regional drills, not regularly scheduled continent-wide exercises.

"Numerous types of civilian and military aircraft were used as mock hijacked aircraft," the statement said. "These exercises tested track detection and identification; scramble and interception; hijack procedures; internal and external agency coordination and operational security and communications security procedures."

"A White House spokesman said Sunday that the Bush administration was not aware of the NORAD exercises. But the exercises using real aircraft show that at least one part of the government thought the possibility of such attacks, though unlikely, merited scrutiny."

88) Training Exercise Held at the White House, Based Around Militants Using a Plane as a Weapon in 1998.

Counter-terrorism expert Richard Clarke chaired an exercise at the White House, which involved the scenario where anti-American militants fill a Lear jet with explosives, and then fly it on a suicide mission towards Washington, D.C. Officials from the Pentagon, Secret Service, and FAA are in attendance, and are asked how they would stop such a threat. Pentagon officials say they could launch fighters from Langley Air Force Base, Virginia.

Amazing how they didn't do that on September 11.

89) U.S. officials had considered the possibility that a hijacked plane could be flown into the main stadium at the 1996 Olympics in Atlanta, Georgia.

"U.S. officials had considered the possibility that a plane could be flown into the main stadium during planning for the 1996 Olympics in Atlanta."

90) A 1998 Federal Report warned the executive branch that Osama bin Laden's terrorists might hijack an airliner and dive bomb it into the Pentagon or other government buildings:

"In 1998, U.S. intelligence had information that a group of unidentified Arabs planned to fly an explosives-laden airplane into the World Trade Center, according to a joint inquiry of the House and Senate intelligence committees.

"The report, which looked at more than a dozen federal intelligence agencies, suggests the United States had more information that might have helped to prevent the terror attacks than the government has previously said.

"It said that in 1998, officials received reports concerning a "bin Laden plot involving aircraft in the New York and Washington, areas." Officials received reports that al Qaeda was trying to establish an operative cell in the United States and that bin Laden was attempting to recruit a group of five to seven young men from the United States to travel to the Middle East for training in conjunction with his plans to strike U.S. domestic targets.

"Government sources told CNN that operative is Khalid Shaikh Mohammed, whom they describe as one of the masterminds of the September 11 attacks. He was indicted by the United States for plotting to bomb U.S. airliners in 1995. Officials believe he also plotted to have airplanes hijacked and flown into U.S. buildings."

91) **"They're going to crash the plane into the World Trade Center."**

The Lone Gunmen, a FOX TV series spin off of *The X-Files*, pilot episode depicted the scenario of 9/11 on March 4, 2001.

In the premiere episode, a secret U.S. Government agency is behind the plot to hijack a Boeing 727, via remote control, and crash it into the World Trade

Center and blame it on foreign terrorists to generate a war for weapon sales and an increase military budget.

"The Cold War's over, John. But with no clear enemy to stock pile against, the arms market's flat. But bring down a fully-loaded 727 into the middle of New York City; you'll find a dozen tin-pot dictators all over the world, just clamoring to take responsibility. And begging to be smart bombed."

"Well, how are they gonna bring it down?"

"Same way a dead man can drive a car."

"Remote access; somebody on the ground's flying your plane."

"Your flight's gonna make an unscheduled stop. In exactly 22 minutes."

"They're going to crash the plane into the World Trade Center."[1]

"I woke up on Sept. 11 and saw it on TV, and the first thing I thought of was The Lone Gunmen," Frank Spotnitz, longtime *X-Files* producer told TV Guide. "But then in the weeks and months that followed, almost no one noticed the connection. What's disturbing about it to me is, you think as a fiction writer that if you can imagine this scenario, then the people in power in the government who are there to imagine disaster scenarios can imagine it, too."[2]

92) Bush, Cheney, Rice and others had all proclaimed that they had never heard of such a plan to use aircraft as

missiles and crash them into buildings.

Condoleezza Rice:

"Nobody in our government, at least, and I don't think the prior government, could envision flying airplanes into buildings on such a massive scale."

"I don't think anybody could have predicted that...they would try to use an airplane as a missile, a hijacked airplane as a missile."[1]

Air Force Gen. Richard Myers -
"You hate to admit it, but we hadn't thought about this."[2]

93) Odigo, a Jewish instant messaging service, warned employees not to go to work on September 11.

Odigo says workers were warned of attack

"Odigo, the instant messaging service, says that two of its workers received messages two hours before the Twin Towers attack on September 11 predicting the attack would happen, and the company has been cooperating with Israeli and American law enforcement, including the FBI, in trying to find the original sender of the message predicting the attack.

"Micha Macover, CEO of the company, said the two

workers received the messages and immediately after the terror attack informed the company's management, which immediately contacted the Israeli security services, which brought in the FBI."

94) Many record companies produced covers and videos portraying the attacks, and also ready to be used as patriotic images before the attacks.

The Coup - Party Music

The Coup had a strong underground fan base, but were not expected to appear on MTV or BET or even to be played on commercial radio stations. So what is the problem? The front album cover which depicted the group front-man, Boots, holding a detonator blowing up the World Trade Center.

Boots spoke about the album and the cover;

"Well, first the album got pulled. Second, people seem to be talking about this because the blast shown in the picture is on the same level and general area of where the planes crashed. When we originally made that picture it was in May and June. It was supposed to be a metaphor to symbolize us destroying 'capitalism'."[1]

Could this album art have been inspired by insider information to boost record sales?

Enrique Iglesias - Hero

Iglesias attributes the success of *Hero* to a combination of good lyrics, melody, and excellent production.

What about, with insider knowledge, the careful planning of releasing this song 3 weeks before a 'terrorist' attack in which heros would certainly arise?

Enrique performed *Hero* for a landmark fund-raiser, *America: A Tribute To Heroes*, aired by all the major networks on September 21, 2001, to raise money for the families of the victims of 9/11. After September 11, this sensitive ballad that became very popular and climbed its way to the third position of the US Singles play-list chart, and hit the top of Billboard's Adult Contemporary and Hot Dance Music/Club Play chart. Hero was also number one in the UK Singles chart. The album, *Escape*, was later certified platinum.

Chrysler then used *Hero* in a commercial for the new 2002 Jeep Liberty, which just happens to be shown driving up the Empire State Building.

95) In August 1997, the US Department of Justice and FEMA, published a self-study course entitled "Emergency Response to Terrorism" with the

following (top) cover:

Only the North Tower of the World Trade Center has a mast.

96) In June 2000, The U.S. Department of Justice brochure "Managing Weapons of Mass Destruction Incidents" again used the 'prophetic' image. (Bottom)

97) **Operation Northwoods**

"In the early 1960s, America's top military leaders reportedly drafted plans to kill innocent people and commit acts of terrorism in U.S. cities to create public support for a war against Cuba.

"Code named Operation

Northwoods, the plans reportedly included the possible assassination of Cuban émigrés, sinking boats of Cuban refugees on the high seas, hijacking planes, blowing up a U.S. ship, and even orchestrating violent terrorism in U.S. cities.

"The plans were developed as ways to trick the American public and the international community into supporting a war to oust Cuba's then new leader, communist Fidel Castro.

"America's top military brass even contemplated causing U.S. military casualties, writing: "We could blow up a U.S. ship in Guantanamo Bay and blame Cuba," and, "casualty lists in U.S. newspapers would cause a helpful wave of national indignation."

"Details of the plans are described in Body of Secrets (Doubleday), a new book by investigative reporter James Bamford about the history of America's largest spy agency, the National Security Agency. However, the plans were not connected to the agency, he notes.

"The plans had the written approval of all of the Joint Chiefs of Staff and were presented to President Kennedy's defense secretary, Robert McNamara, in March 1962. But they apparently were rejected by the civilian leadership and have gone undisclosed for nearly 40 years.

"The Joint Chiefs even proposed using the potential death of astronaut John Glenn during the first attempt to put an American into orbit as a false pretext for war with Cuba, the documents show.

7. Hijacking attempts against civil air and surface craft should appear to continue as harassing measures condoned by the government of Cuba. Concurrently, genuine defections of Cuban civil and military air and surface craft should be encouraged.

8. It is possible to create an incident which will demonstrate convincingly that a Cuban aircraft has attacked and shot down a chartered civil airliner enroute from the United States to Jamaica, Guatemala, Panama or Venezuela. The destination would be chosen only to cause the flight plan route to cross Cuba. The passengers could be a group of college students off on a holiday or any grouping of persons with a common interest to support chartering a non-scheduled flight.

a. An aircraft at Eglin AFB would be painted and numbered as an exact duplicate for a civil registered aircraft belonging to a CIA proprietary organization in the Miami area. At a designated time the duplicate would be substituted for the actual civil aircraft and would be loaded with the selected passengers, all boarded under
_____ _____ _____ The actual registered

"Should the rocket explode and kill Glenn, they wrote, "the objective is to provide irrevocable proof … that the fault lies with the Communists et all Cuba."

"The plans were motivated by an intense desire among senior military leaders to depose Castro, who seized power in 1959 to become the first communist leader in the Western Hemisphere — only 90 miles from U.S. shores.

"The earlier CIA-backed Bay of Pigs invasion of Cuba by Cuban exiles had been a disastrous failure, in which the military was not allowed to provide firepower. The military leaders now wanted a shot at it.

"Reflecting this, the U.S. plan called for establishing prolonged military — not democratic — control over the island nation after the invasion.

"The Joint Chiefs at the time were headed by Eisenhower appointee Army Gen. Lyman L. Lemnitzer, who, with the signed plans in hand made a pitch to McNamara on March 13, 1962, recommending Operation Northwoods be run by the military.

"Whether the Joint Chiefs' plans were rejected by McNamara in the meeting is not clear. But three days later, President Kennedy told Lemnitzer directly there was virtually no possibility of ever using overt force to take Cuba, Bamford reports. Within months, Lemnitzer would be denied another term as chairman and transferred to another job.

"The secret plans came at a time when there was distrust in the military leadership about their civilian leadership, with leaders in the Kennedy administration viewed as too liberal, insufficiently experienced and soft on communism. At the same time, however, there real were concerns in American society about their military overstepping its bounds.

"There were reports U.S. military leaders had encouraged their subordinates to vote conservative during the election.

"And at least two popular books were published focusing on a right-wing military leadership pushing the limits against government policy of the day. The Senate Foreign Relations Committee published its own report on right-wing extremism in the military, warning a "considerable danger" in the "education and propaganda activities of military personnel" had been uncovered. The committee even called for an examination of any ties between Lemnitzer and right-wing groups. But Congress didn't get wind of Northwoods, says Bamford.

"Even after Lemnitzer was gone, he writes, the Joint Chiefs continued to plan "pretext" operations at least through 1963.

"One idea was to create a war between Cuba and another Latin American country so that the United States could intervene. Another was to pay someone in the Castro government to attack U.S. forces at the Guantanamo naval base — an act, which Bamford notes, would have amounted to treason. And another was to fly low level U-2 flights over Cuba, with the intention of having one shot down as a pretext for a war.

"Afraid of a congressional investigation, Lemnitzer had ordered all Joint Chiefs documents related to the Bay of Pigs destroyed, says Bamford. But somehow, these remained."

And the scenario played out on September 11, 2001.

98) The New American Century

As the cold war ended, and the fall of Communism rose, enemies were hard to find.

When George W. Bush was sworn into office in January 2001, he brought with him many of the distinguished voices and members of the neo-conservative movement within the Republican Party. Many of which whom served along side the Ronald Regan and George H. W. Bush administrations:

PROJECT FOR THE

NEW AMERICAN CENTURY

Richard "Dick" Cheney, Donald Rumsfield, Collin Powell, and Paul Wolfowitz.

In September 2000, these neo-conservative think tanks founded a proposed strategy titled "Rebuilding America's Defenses" published by "The Project of a New American Century."

This proposal called on the United States to increase "the military budget to be raised 100 billion dollars," to "Deny others the use of (outer) space," to preemptively "Shape circumstances before crises arise," and to "boldly and purposefully promote

70

American principles abroad."

It also called for the elimination of "States like Iraq"

They admitted:

"Since the Cold War is over, the report said, we don't have that excuse to keep military spending up.

"Therefore, according to the report, any transformation of military affairs will go rather slowly, absent some catastrophic and catalyzing event like a New Pearl Harbor."

One year later, the Project for a New American Century got this event. . .

According to *The Washington Post*, before going to bed, President Bush wrote in his diary, "The Pearl Harbor of the 21st century took place today."

99) Remember, that Muslims were blamed for the first WTC bombing in October of 1993.

The bomber, a 43 year old Egyptian Emad Salem, admitted to the courts that he was paid one million dollars and trained by the FBI.

According to Salem's testimony and stories in the *New York Times*, the FBI had told him it was only a terrorism drill.

When the FBI had given Salem real explosives he realized he was being set up and secretly recorded his conversations with the FBI.

John Anticev, a top official in the FBI, is one of the men on these recordings and he is heard telling Salem to proceed with the bombing.

Sadly this story faded away and the American public is unaware of the true engineers behind the first WTC attack.

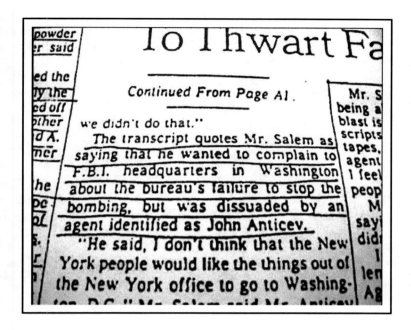

To Thwart Fa

Continued From Page A1.

powder
r said

ed the
ty the
ed off
other
d X.
ner

he
De
of

s.
r
n

we didn't do that."
The transcript quotes Mr. Salem as
saying that he wanted to complain to
F.B.I. headquarters in Washington
about the bureau's failure to stop the
bombing, but was dissuaded by an
agent identified as John Anticev.
"He said, I don't think that the New
York people would like the things out of
the New York office to go to Washington D.C." Mr. Salem said Mr. Anticev

Mr. S
being a
blast is
scripts
tapes,
agent
I feel
peop
M
say
did
1
len
Ag

100) A 1995 card game titled *Illuminati: New World Order* contains cards that bear striking resemblances to the events that occurred on September 11.

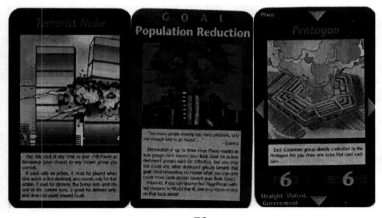

101) Osama bin Laden stated on 9/11

"I tell you, freedom and human rights in America are doomed. The U.S. Government will lead the American people - and the West in general - into an unbearable hell and chocking life." - *BBC*

"When you eliminate the impossible, whatever remains – however improbable – must be the truth!"
- Doyle

Dear Readers,

There are more than 101 points that prove that the American public, and the people of the world, are the victims of a horrible hoax.

Although there are many websites available, please check out:

www.rense.com
www.whatreallyhappened.com
www.davidicke.com
www.letsroll911.org
http://killtown.911review.org
www.physics911.net
www.reopen911.org

There are also hundreds of great books as well. I welcome you to read my books as well as:

Alice in Wonderland and the World Trade Center Disaster by David Icke

The New Pearl Harbor and *The 9/11 Commission Report: Omissions and Distortions* by David Ray Griffin

As Osama bin Laden stated "I tell you, freedom and human rights in America are doomed. The U.S. Government will lead the American people - and the West in general - into an unbearable hell and chocking life."

And President Bush declared that the terrorists are attacking "America's way of life and our freedom."

Ask yourself, 'Was it Osama bin Laden who has legislated away your freedom?' Or, 'Was it the people placed in office who swore a oath to protect it?'

If the people will lead, the leaders will follow.

The time is now to take back the country!

Please check out my website, www.whatreallyisthematrix.com for updates and information how you can start by taking back your country.

Let the truth, begin with you.

Eric D. Williams
morpheus@whatreallyisthematrix.com
www.whatreallyisthematrix.com

Sources

1) http://911research.wtc7.net/planes/evidence/passengers.html
2) http://archives.cnn.com/2001/US/09/21/inv.id.theft/)
3) 1- http://www.cnn.com/SPECIALS/2001/trade.center/victims/
   AA11.victims.html
   2- http://www.usatoday.com/news/nation/2001/09/11/victims
   -list.htm
   3- The Puzzle of 9-11 by Eric D. Williams
4) http://a188.g.akamaitech.net/f/188/920/15m/www.washington
   post.com/wp-srv/nation/graphics/hijack091101.htm
5) Ibid
6) Ibid
7) Ibid
8) 1- http://news.bbc.co.uk/hi/english/world/middle_east/newsid
   _1559000/1559151.stm
   2- http://www.mujahideen.fsnet.co.uk/wtc/wtc-hijackers.htm
9) 1- http://en.wikipedia.org/wiki/Mohamed_Atta_al_Sayed
   2- http://www.americanfreepress.net/html/new_questions
   _about.html
10) http://en.wikipedia.org/wiki/Mohamed_Atta_al_Sayed
11) 1- http://archives.cnn.com/2001/US/09/13/flight.schools/
    2- http://edition.cnn.com/2001/US/09/12/investigation.terrorism/
12) 1- http://en.wikipedia.org/wiki/Mohamed_Atta_al_Sayed
    2- St. Petersburg Times (09/13/01)
    http://www.sptimes.com/News/091301/Worldandnation/FBI_
    seizes_records_of.shtml
13) 1- http://www.noradsanta.org
    2- http://www.norad.org
14) Meyers Confirmation Testimony, Senate Armed Services
    Committee, Washington, September 13, 2001
15) http://www.attackonamerica.net/didhijackersflythroughholesinusa
    irdefense.htm
16) Ibid
17) 'Loss of Oxygen Cited as Possible Cause of Jet's Wayward Flight,
    Crash'
    Lynn Lunsford 10/26/1999

KRTBN Knight-Ridder Tribune Business News: The Dallas Morning News - Texas

18) http://www.abovetopsecret.com/forum/thread17588/pg1
19) Ibid
    Boston Globe, September 15, 2001
20) http://inn.globalfreepress.com/modules/news/article.php?
    storyid=858
21) http://www.transtats.bts.gov/
22) Please view *In Plane Site* available at
    http://www.thepowerhour.com/
23) Fox News 9-11-01 also available on In Plane Site mentioned
    above
24) http://www.rense.com/general63/hiding.htm
25) http://www.freerepublic.com/focus/f-news/520255/posts
26) 9/11 Naude Documentary
27) http://www.cnn.com/TRANSCRIPTS/0112/04/se.04.html
28) http://history1900s.about.com/library/misc/blempirecrash.htm
29) 1- http://www.sarasotamagazine.com/pages/hotstories/hotstories.
    asp?136
    2- http://observer.guardian.co.uk/print/0,3858,4258186
    -102275,00.html
30) http://www.rense.com/general63/pm.htm
    http://www.dfrc.nasa.gov/gallery/photo/CID/HTML/index.html
    http://www.911wasalie.com/phpwebsite/index.php?module
    =announce&ANN_user_op=view&ANN_id=25
31) http://www.aircrash.org/burnelli/ht960724.htm
    By Fred Bayles The Associated Press, International Hearld
    Tribune - Wednesday, July 24, 1996
32) http://www.aviewoncities.com/nyc/wtc.htm
33) Ibid
34) 1-http://www.lafire.com/famous_fires/880504_1stInterstateFire
    /050488_InterstateFire.htm
    2- http://globalresearch.ca.myforums.net/viewtopic.php?t=835
    3- http://www.cnn.com/2005/WORLD/europe/02/13/spain.
    block.fire
35) http://www.wallofamericans.com/index2.html
36) PBS Documentary America Rebuilds
37) http://www.mindfully.org/Reform/2004/Larry-Silverstein-
    WTC6dec04.htm

38) 1- Encyclopedia Britannica
2- http://www.bushstole04.com/9-11-01_new_6b.htm
39) http://www.bushstole04.com/9-11-01_new_6b.htm
40) Ibid
41) Self-Evident
42) "The Collapse: An Engineer's Perspective," NOVA interview
with Thomas Eagar
(www.pbs.org/wgbh/nova/wtc/collapse.html)
43) Self-Evident
http://www.webelements.com/webelements/elements/text/Fe/heat.html
44) 1- http://www.rense.com/general17/eyewitnessreportspersist.htm
2- http://www.boeing.com/commercial/707family/
3- http://www.boeing.com/commercial/767family/pf/pf_
200prod.html
45) Self-Evident
46) People Weekly Magazine, September 24, 2001
47) http://english.pravda.ru/columnists/2002/07/25/33228_.html
48) Self-Evident
49) *9/11* Naduet Brothers Documentary Film
50) http://www.arcticbeacon.com/articles/article/1518131/28031.htm
51) Self-Evident
52) http://www.rense.com/general68/mreproof.htm
53) http://www.whatreallyhappened.com/911security.html
54) http://www.washingtonpost.com/wp-srv/metro/daily/sep01/attack.
html
55) 1- http://www.wtc7.net/steeldisposal.html
2- FEMA's Report #403, *World Trade Center Building
Perfomance Study,*
available at: www.fema.gov/library/wtcstudy.shtm
56) http://www.boeing.com/commercial/757family/pf/pf_200tech.
html
57) Self-Evident
58) Self-Evident
59) Self-Evident
60) http://www.cnn.com/2001/US/09/11/pentagon.terrorism/
61) http://www.boeing.com/commercial/757family/pf/pf_200tech.
html
62) http://www.cbsnews.com/stories/2001/09/11/national/main310721
.shtml

63) Self-Evident

64) Self-Evident

65) http://www.fas.org/man/dod-101/sys/smart/agm-86c.htm

66) http://a188.g.akamaitech.net/f/188/920/5m/www.washingtonpost.
com/wp-srv/metro/daily/sep01/attack.html

67) CNN, September 11, 2001
http://thewebfairy.com/911/pentagon/index.html

68) http://www.the7thfire.com/9-11/911_has_shown_the_face_of_N
WO.htm

69) http://www.defenselink.mil/news/Nov2001/t11182001_t1012pm.
html

70) http://www.af.mil/factsheets/factsheet_print.asp?fsID=175&page
=1

71) http://www.sierratimes.com/03/07/02/article_tro.htm

72) http://feralnews.com/issues/911/dewdney/project_achilles_report_
2_030225.html

73) 1- http://www.flight93crash.com/
2- http://home.comcast.net/~skydrifter/flt93.htm

74) http://www.flight93crash.com/second-plane-at-flight93-crash-site.
htm

75) Self-Evident

76) http://www.renewamerica.us/columns/kovach/051012

77) http://www.rense.com/general68/says.html

78) http://www.rense.com/general68/911h.htm

79) http://www.whitehouse.gov/news/releases/2001/09/printi2001090
7-1.html

80) 1- According to the 9/11 Commission, Chief of Staff Andrew
Card, the lead Secret Service agent, the president's military
aide, and Air Force One pilot Colonel Mark Tillman, discuss a
possible destination for Air Force One after take off.
According to a Daily Telegraph article, President Bush spent
most of his time at Barksdale Air Force Base arguing over the
phone with Vice President Dick Cheney over where he should go
next. "A few minutes before 1 p.m.," he agreed to fly to Nebraska.
There were also rumors of a "credible terrorist threat" to Air Force
One that are said to prevent his return to Washington.
http://www.telegraph.co.uk/news/main.jhtml?xml=/news/2001/12/
16/wbush16.xml
Eventually, the plane leaves Sarasota Florida, to Barksdale,

Louisiana, then departs to Offutt, Nebraska
before finally arriving in Washington, D.C.
2- CNN 09/11/01, Washington Times,
www.washtimes.com/national/20010911-21577384.htm

81)   1- **SEC Probes Suspicious Trading**, by Marcy Gordon, *The Associated Press*, October 2, 2001
       2- **More Unusual Market Activity Reported Before Attacks**, by Laura Jacobs and Thomas Atkins, *Reuters*, September 20, 2001
       3- **Suspicious profits sit uncollected Airline investors seem to be lying low**, by Christian Berthelsen, and Scott Winokur, *San Francisco Chronicle*, September 29, 2001
       4- **Treasury Bonds Enter Purview of U.S. Inquiry Into Attack Gains**, by Charles Gasparino and Gregory Zuckerman, *The Wall Street Journal*, October 2, 2001

82)   1- CBS News, July 26, 2001.
       http://www.cbsnews.com/stories/2001/07/26/national/
       main303601.shtml
       See also the 9/11 Commission Report
       2- **Willie Brown got low-key early warning about air travel**, by Phillip Matier and Andrew Ross, *San Francisco Chronicle* , September 12, 2001
       3- **Rushdie's Air Ban**, by James Doran, *Times* (London), September 27, 2001

83)   1- **Some Got Warning: Don't Go Downtown on Sept. 11**, by Greg B. Smith, *The New York Daily News*, October 12, 2001
       2- Ibid
       3- **Seattle man reportedly warned of terror attack** , by Sam Skolnik, Seattle Post - Intelligence, October 12, 2001
       4- http://www.villagevoice.com/issues/0239/goodyear.php

84)   *CBS Evening News with Dan Rather*, September 12, 2001
       A recording of this conversation can be heard online at
       http://www.whatreallyhappened.com/fema.rm

85)   http://www.infowars.com/saved%20pages/Prior_Knowledge/
       sitting_on_theFBI.htm

86)   http://www.globalnewsmatrix.com/modules.php?name=
       News&file=article&sid=2632

87)   http://www.usatoday.com/news/washington/2004-04-18-
       norad_x.htm

88)   *9/11 Commission Final Report*, 7/24/04, pp. 345 & 457-458

89) *Star-Ledger*, 5/24/03

90) http://fyi.cnn.com/2002/ALLPOLITICS/09/18/intelligence.
hearings/

91) 1- http://www.thewebfairy.com/killtown/lonegunmen.html
2- http://kjbbn.net/gunmen_foreshadowed_911.htm

92) 1- Rice CBS, 05/17/02
2- Myers Department of Defense October, 23, 2001

93) http://www.haaretzdaily.com/hasen/pages/ShArt.jhtml?itemNo=7
7744&contrassID=/has%5C

94) 1- http://www.daveyd.com/bootsonthewarpolitics.html
2- http://auditionsearch.com/bios/enrique_iglesias.htm

95) http://www.the7thfire.com/Politics%20and%20History/FEMA-on
-Target.html

96) http://www.thememoryhole.org/911/managing-wmd.htm

97) ABC News 05/01/01
http://abcnews.go.com/US/story?id=92662&page=1 Northwoods

98) http://www.newamericancentury.org/RebuildingAmericas
Defenses.pdf
http://www.newamericancentury.org/
Bush New Pearl Harbor -
http://www.washingtonpost.com/ac2/wp-dyn/A42754-2002Jan26

99) *The New York Times*, October 28, 1993 and October 31, 1993
The Chicago Tribune, December 15, 1993

100) Steve Jackson Games http://www.sjgames.com/inwo/

101) Osama bin Laden, Al-Jazeera interview, Oct 21, 2001;
also reported on CNN's Wolf Blitzer reports, Jan 31, 2002

Also from Eric D. Williams

The Puzzle of 9-11:
An investigation into the events of September 11, 2001,
and why the pieces don't fit together
ISBN 1-4196-0033-8

The Puzzle of the Matrix:
Intriguing explorations into the nature of reality
ISBN 1-4196-0504-6

Now Available:
The Puzzle of Fascism:
Could fascism arise in America or could it already be a
Fascist State?
ISBN 1-4196-3255-8

www.whatreallyisthematrix.com